DIGITAL CITIZENSHIP AND YOU™

DIGITAL ETHICS
SAFE AND LEGAL BEHAVIOR ONLINE

AMIE JANE LEAVITT

Rosen
YA™

New York

Published in 2019 by The Rosen Publishing Group, Inc.
29 East 21st Street, New York, NY 10010

Library of Congress Cataloging-in-Publication Data

Names: Leavitt, Amie Jane, author.
Title: Digital ethics : safe and legal behavior online / Amie Jane
Leavitt.
Description: New York : Rosen Publishing, 2019 | Series: Digital
citizenship and you | Audience: Grades 7–12. | Includes bibli-
ographical references and index.
Identifiers: LCCN 2018021591| ISBN 9781508184577 (library
bound) | ISBN 9781508184560 (pbk.)
Subjects: LCSH: Internet—Moral and ethical aspects—Juvenile
literature. | Internet—Social aspects—Juvenile literature. | Internet
users—Psychology—Juvenile literature.
Classification: LCC HM851 .L43 2019 | DDC 302.23/1—dc23
LC record available at https://lccn.loc.gov/2018021591

Manufactured in the United States of America

CONTENTS

INTRODUCTION

Imagine you just got home. It's been a long day of school and extracurriculars, and all you feel like doing is decompressing in your room by going online. You pull out a phone, tablet, or laptop and start scrolling through your feeds. Perhaps you click the Like button on a few of the posts: one shows a friend on vacation with her family and another shows a relative eating a delicious-looking meal at a restaurant.

If you keep on scrolling, imagine coming across a negative post, perhaps making fun of someone for how that person looks or who he or she is. How do you react? Do you give it a Like and move on? Or maybe you chime in with a sarcastic, witty remark? Maybe you challenge the poster by sending that person a direct message, telling him or her to step back. There are many routes to take. It's not always easy to know what to do in situations like these. The online world is a vast and impressive space, full of many interconnected, online communities. We must tread lightly, though, because there are real people behind the posts and photos we see and comment on.

Scenarios like this occur online daily. People encounter things on the internet, including on social media, with which they don't feel comfortable. However, instead of doing something about it, like standing up for a person being targeted and speaking out on that person's

Without ethics to guide us, living our day-to-day lives online would sometimes be confusing and discouraging.

behalf, many people do nothing. Or, even worse, they sometimes pile on to or otherwise contribute to online harassment, intimidation, and other abuse.

One thing people draw upon when deciding how to interact with others is their own personal set of ethics. So, what exactly are ethics? And how can they be applied to the decisions that we make? In this book, we will explore these questions and issues.

Before exploring the ins and outs of interacting ethically with others online, we must ask ourselves what it means to be part of the online community. As in real life, the things we do online are part of who we are. Citizens in the real world vote, work, go to school, and otherwise enter situations that may challenge their ethical perspectives.

Whether one is learning, participating in social media, or making money, good digital citizenship tends to make things smoother and easier on the internet. The internet is a great tool that empowers learning and problem solving. It also allows us to build communities, both locally and globally, with whom we can establish connections via hobbies, games, socializing, art, commerce, and other forms of engagement and collaboration. Beefing up on what digital ethics entail can only help digital denizens be better digital citizens—whether they are digital natives who have grown up online, or relative newcomers online.

CHAPTER ONE

OUR MORAL COMPASS

The word "ethics" originates from the Greek word *ethos* which means "custom, habit, character, or disposition." Systems of ethics help us define the concepts of right and wrong. A system of ethics serves as a person's moral compass. Living according to one can provide standards of behavior and help a person figure out questions of conscience. There are many cases where ethics allow us to weigh different options on how to act, and in doing so they encourage us to live better lives and to respect others and ourselves.

Ethics help human beings answer fundamental questions. Asking ethical questions can provide a moral map for our lives and help us navigate important decisions when they arise. They examine our obligations to ourselves and others. They also allow us to determine who we are and our character.

- What are my principles?
- What are my values?
- What do I stand for?
- What can I do versus what should I do?

This bust depicts Socrates, the Greek philosopher who thought deeply about ethical issues and problems, and whose influence still remains strong in modern ethics.

To behave ethically means to treat others with respect and avoid harming others. It means not lying, cheating, or stealing. For some, it goes hand in hand with treating others how you would like to be treated.

IN EVERY FIELD

Ethics doesn't just deal with individuals. It also determines the behavior, conduct, and actions of organizations, companies, and governments. There are ethical standards and systems in every field today, including business, law, the military, health care, scientific and medical research, character education, the environment, government, journalism, leadership, religion, sports, technology, engineering, and so forth.

For example, business ethics deal with proper behavior in the workplace and proper actions by a company. Should employees disclose conflicts of interest to their employer? How should employees behave while on the job? How should a company do business? What kinds of products should they make? How should a company treat its employees? How should a company acquire raw materials for products? These are just some of the questions that might arise.

Scientific research is another field with its own ethical considerations, especially when human and animal subjects are concerned. The ethics of biomedical research include the answers to such questions as: Should a doctor be allowed to do a study on a patient without that person's consent? What should be done

Disgraced former chief executive officer (CEO) Kenneth Lay takes the oath during a Senate hearing on the massive fraud at his company, the energy giant Enron, which collapsed in 2001.

with genetic information? Should a company be allowed to test products on animals to make sure they are safe for humans?

As you may have noticed, ethical questions often deal with things one should do, rather those that they can, or are allowed, to do. That's because technically a person or organization can do many things and can choose among any number of courses of action. However, when the question is changed to "should," the topic is now looked at ethically and people are permitting the needle of a moral compass to determine their course of action.

ETHICS IN AN ONLINE WORLD

Another branch of ethics, sometimes known as digital ethics, focuses specifically on behavior and activities in the online world. It takes into consideration the rights and wrongs of online behavior and activities. These are any actions (or lack thereof) of individuals, organizations, companies, governments, and so forth.

Digital ethics considers many different issues. How should people treat each other online? Should a person download media without paying for it? How should a person respond when he or she realizes someone else is being bullied? Can internet users post whatever they want online? What about spreading false information or pretending they are someone else? Should companies be able to harvest user data? What about revealing secrets or confidential information online about others (individuals, organizations, companies, or governments)? What regulations should companies or governments be able to impose on online activity?

Digital citizens face as many ethical dilemmas as people do in real life. Consequences in the real world have, thus far, been more specifically defined. At the same time, much of real life now has an online component. This includes employment, banking, forging relationships, dating, shopping, political organizing and advocacy, and many more aspects of modern life. Rules, regulations, and the legal dimensions of online behavior are still catching up to those we have long established, before there was even an online world to speak of.

IN REAL LIFE VERSUS THE ONLINE WORLD

Many experiences one has online can be anonymous. It is often difficult to tell if someone's screen persona matches who they are "in real life," (or IRL). Anonymity can sometimes bring out the worst in people. They may attempt things online that they would never do in person. They may mistreat people, deceive people, engage in dishonest behavior, spread false information, or take things that don't belong to them. For those who would do bad things, the internet has enabled them to do these things faster, more efficiently, and sometimes with less fear of consequences. As the twenty-first century progresses, the boundaries between these two worlds have become increasingly blurred.

The speed of technology often outpaces debate over the ethical concerns surrounding its uses. Hackers and other unsavory characters online are one symptom of this problem.

Technology has developed so quickly that regular people, ethicists, technologists, and lawmakers have struggled to keep up. In some cases, this has created a "Wild West" or "anything goes" mentality surrounding online culture. Every new application, or app, that is created, along with every new device or platform, seems to present its own sets of benefits, drawbacks, and ethical concerns.

DIGITAL COMMUNITIES

The online world isn't going anywhere; in fact, it will likely become more important in our lives. Because of that,

ETHICS IN TECHNOLOGY AND ENGINEERING: IS DRONE USAGE ETHICAL?

Drones are an example of a new technology whose use has sparked debate about right and wrong. Proponents of drones believe they are valuable tools for law enforcement and the military. They believe they can be helpful in many fields, from media and broadcasting, to agriculture, traffic control, and other applications.

However, just like any other technology, drone use can be abused. For instance, should people be able to use drones for whatever reason they want? Should they be able to photograph and video any place, event, or group of people that they want? What about when governments are able to use drones to spy on people indiscriminately? What are the rights of drone users compared to the airspace needs of pilots, airline passengers, and those who handle security and safety? How about people who do not want themselves recorded or their privacy invaded?

All of these questions, and more, have come about because of the invention of drones. And they're still being debated and legislated. For example, laws have been passed which prohibit the use of drones near airports or over crowded sporting events. These are called "no-drone fly zones." However, it's very difficult to enforce such laws. Drones are small and fast, which makes it a challenge for law enforcement to accurately detect who was flying the drone. Much more will need to be done to provide for the greatest use of this technology while protecting the rights and safety of people, groups, and countries.

everyone must evaluate the type of online world that they want to create. Do people want spaces that are safe, inviting, and encouraging where everyone feels welcome to participate, learn, and improve? Or do they want to create something very different? It's all up to members of the online community.

In every community, there are citizens or residents of that community. In the online world, digital citizens are also called netizens. As netizens, people must grapple with very complex issues when it comes to online behavior. For instance, should the internet to be a place where people can say and do anything they

British cybercriminal Marcus Hutchins , shown at right walking with his attorneys in August 2017, was actually a security expert accused of spreading malware to crack victims' banking passwords.

want? Or should the internet have limits, just like in the real world? If so, how do netizens impose those limits? How do they make sure there are consequences for online behavior? How do they come up with rules for people who are from all kinds of political and geographical boundaries, and then enforce those rules?

It can seem overwhelming to look at the big picture of online ethics. To really bring it home, we must drill down to individual choices and scenarios. You might ask yourself what your values, principles, and ideals are in the real world, and how do you make sure to adhere to them when you're online.

CHAPTER TWO

DO NO HARM

One key principle of ethical behavior is derived from an old Latin expression, *Primum non nocere*, which translates to "first, do no harm." It is a rule that is mostly identified with ethics in medicine. But it can also broadly be applied to many human interactions. This means avoiding harming individuals, groups, companies, nations—even the earth itself. In digital ethics, this can mean not actively trying to hurt others, contributing somehow to others doing so, or causing someone harm due to one's inaction or neglect.

DON'T BE A BULLY

Bullying did not suddenly spring up in the era of the internet. It certainly is not something that happens exclusively online. If you pick any film, television show, book, or other creative work that takes place in a school setting, it is a good bet that a bully will arise as a major figure or character for the main characters to deal with,

Bullying and harassment in person are not very different from these same behaviors online. The latter can sometimes be even more traumatizing.

and hopefully overcome. One classic bully is the character of Biff Tannen from the 1985 film *Back to the Future.* In the entire film franchise, the villainous Biff is the quintessential bully who constantly picks on the heroes. He never grows out of his bullying nature, even as he becomes an adult.

Unfortunately, real-life bullies are found everywhere, from childhood through old age. Bullies exist in school, the workplace, politics, and every community. Sadly, this is because some people never reach or internalize the moral development that allows them to have and show empathy for others. Many choose not to, while others never see such behavior as an option.

As a result, some people can turn out to be seventy-year-old Biffs who demean, criticize, and make fun of others. But this behavior doesn't just hurt the victims of bullying—it can also hurt bullies. They may get into trouble that hurts their educational and professional careers, and can alienate any friends they have, as well as family and others in the community. Many bullies might have emotional and developmental issues, be victims of abuse at home, or otherwise be unable to deal with others constructively.

BULLYING ONLINE

Bullying that occurs online—otherwise known as cyberbullying—has been in the news a lot these days. Cyberbullying is hurting, intimidating, or threatening another person, often repeatedly, using a computer, smartphone, or other electronic device. Cyberbullying is identified mostly with teens and preteens, but people of all ages engage in it. It can include the following actions:

- Spreading rumors about others online or through texts
- Posting embarrassing pictures of people on social media or texting such images
- Pretending to be someone else in order to trick, lead on, or hurt another person (also known as catfishing)
- Sending mean, hostile, or threatening messages to another person
- Creating a website or social media page with the sole purpose of making fun of someone

- Tricking someone into sharing personal photos or information and then sharing the photos or information with others, specifically to embarrass or silence that person
- Researching someone online, finding out that person's real identity, and then posting his or her personal information online so others can harass him or her (also known as doxxing), even exposing the person to potential death threats
- Forwarding private text messages to others
- Ganging up when others are bullying someone (also known as a pile-on)

Young people who bully, harass, or stalk others online often have little empathy for their victims, who can suffer both short- and long-term harmful consequences from being targeted.

COUNTERING CYBERBULLYING

Claire Kouns was no stranger to bullying. Some bullies gravitated to her because of a speech impediment arising from her hearing loss. However, Claire explained her decision to turn the other cheek during an interview with a Houston ABC affiliate, "Maybe those people that were picking on me were going through a hard time and they're just letting it out on me." Kouns believed that if she replied with kindness rather than anger, it could make them stop. She also had compassion for others who were victims of bullying. In the fall of 2014, her compassion for everyone inspired her to make a difference at her high school near Houston, Texas.

Kouns knew of one student in particular, Kailyn Wallace, who had often been singled out, called names, and mocked for her weight and appearance. The onslaught began to affect Wallace's self-opinion and well-being. Kouns wanted Wallace to know that others saw her as a beautiful person, too. Hence, she decided to anonymously post a nice picture she had of Wallace on the high school's Instagram page. She added a personal message declaring, "You're beautiful . . . What those people said about you wasn't right!" She also continued to anonymously post about other students. People started to notice. Wallace felt happy that someone would do something so sweet for her.

Other students remarked at how important they felt it was that someone was spreading positivity at school. Kouns felt the power that positivity could do for both recipient and giver. "It makes me pretty happy to know people are happy from something I'm saying," she proudly explained to reporters during the television interview. Standing up to bullying nonviolently, turning the other cheek, and pretty much any way that helps young people deal with and overcome the problem are all valid copings techniques.

One of the biggest problems with online bullying is that there's often no escape from it, especially for kids and teens, who are particularly vulnerable to this type of treatment. These days, the internet is everywhere. Cyberbullies can attack all day and all night whether the victim is at school, home, or even when they're asleep or away on vacation. Because of that, victims of cyberbullying are left feeling very hopeless, alone, humiliated, worthless, and without a friend in the world. Cyberbullying can lead to anxiety, depression, and in the worst cases, even suicide.

Cyberbullying isn't funny or just something that "people do" to be cool or popular. It's one of the most unethical ways to behave online. People who fall into the trap of cyberbullying others need to stop immediately, apologize, and make amends for their actions when possible.

TROLLING AND ETHICS

Trolling is another form of unethical online behavior. It is a behavior meant to rile up others online. It is accomplished by posting offensive comments or other disruptive content, including seemingly nonsensical posts. Trolls lurk in the comments section of websites, in discussions on all sorts of topics on social media, in chat rooms, in game forums, via private messaging, and pretty much anywhere else online that people have the ability to interact with each other.

Trolls's main goals are to cause trouble online. They like to start arguments and fights and get people angry, upset, or sad. According to psychologists, one of the reasons that trolls troll is because they feel that they can. In an online environment, sometimes people feel less inhibited when they're hiding behind a screen (computer, smart phone, tablet, and any other electronic device). While they get an illicit thrill from seeing the effects of their trolling on a certain level, some trolls do not realize nor internalize the actual harm they cause others.

With this feeling of anonymity or security that fake names and distance from other users provides, people can sometimes act very differently online than they would otherwise. This is where ethics come into play. If a person would never do something in real life because

Social media networks like Facebook have helped connect people, but they have also created online environments that are ripe for trolling and other abusive behaviors.

of their innate beliefs and ethical values, then they certainly shouldn't behave that way online.

THE PROS AND CONS OF ANONYMITY

Many people choose to do things anonymously online. Anonymity can be used for good, as well for ill. It all depends on why someone chooses to remain anonymous. A pro of anonymity is that people can do nice things for others and let the author remain a mystery. In a situation like Claire Kouns's, where she posted anonymous photos and positive comments about fellow classmates, the anonymity worked to everyone's favor. Since no one knew who was doing these positive acts, a general sense of goodwill was created among all the students at the school.

Another big advantage of anonymity is that people can get involved in online communities that provide specific help and support without fear of embarrassment or unwanted publicity. For example, there are groups and forums that help people with private matters like addiction, depression, and gender identity issues. By concealing their identity, people can get real help and guidance from people without the fear of being ridiculed, condemned, or harmed by people in the real world who are unsympathetic to their difficulties.

The ability to conceal one's identity online also creates problems. People can sometimes act out and veer into abusive behavior. Because they are hiding behind a cloak of secrecy, they might say and do things that they wouldn't normally do in the real world. Unfortunately, many of those words and actions can be quite negative. That's where a code of ethics helps a person regardless of their situation. It's what you do and say when you think no one else is looking that truly reflects on your character. That especially includes behavior behind an anonymous Twitter handle, or other social media account.

There are many opinions out there for how to best deal with trolls. Here are a few ways that some experts recommend:

1. **Don't Feed the Trolls**. Trolls often want attention. So, if you ignore them, they just might stop. Besides, giving attention to only positive ideas and thoughts might breed more positivity.
2. **Block, Block, and Block**. There's no need to follow someone or let that person follow you if he or she is going to troll. If trolling happens on social media, then block that person and delete his or her comments from your photo or page. You should report him or her if you feel the comments could pose harm to others (or yourself).
3. **Gather Evidence**. Screenshot the comments if you feel that they need to be reported to moderators or website administrators, or admins. If the trolling happens on your own page, share the information with a trusted adult like a family member, teacher, coach, or counselor. These people

can offer guidance and provide help that you may need to deal with such situations.

4. **Don't Troll**. If you find yourself being negative or mean online, check yourself! Ask yourself this question: if the person were sitting right here by me, would I still say that to his or her face? If the answer is no, then you should definitely not post the comment online.

Sometimes, the most straightforward fix to avoid or shut down a harasser is to block that person, on Twitter or other sites.

THE GOLDEN RULE

Sometimes people purposely do things to hurt other people (bullying), but other times people do things that hurt others without really trying to hurt them. For example, posting a picture of a friend that another mutual friend thinks is funny is a common enough action. What if such a post goes viral throughout the school community and everyone sees it? This might make the third friend a laughingstock and even cause that friend to be bullied and otherwise harassed.

Always remember that someone might not intend to act maliciously and end up hurting someone else. During times like these, digital citizens need to check themselves and think about the consequences of their behavior, however minuscule they appear to be ahead of time. They must ask themselves, "Would I like it if someone did this to me?" If the answer is no, then they definitely shouldn't do it.

CHAPTER THREE

PROTECTING YOURSELF ONLINE

In a perfect world, everyone would act ethically and we would not have to be concerned about protecting ourselves. But that is certainly not the case in the real world or online. Because of that, we must follow guidelines and take necessary steps to stay safe in all of our online pursuits.

THINK BEFORE YOU POST

One of the best ways to stay safe online is to simply think before you post. Let's say you want to share a picture of yourself because you think that only certain people will be able to see it. Perhaps you want to make a joke or funny comment, share a questionable meme, or post a video because only your friends or followers have access to it. Think twice. A good rule of thumb is if you would be embarrassed to have your parents, teachers, principal, members of the community, or even law enforcement see the post, then you probably should not post that content.

Always be aware that one's online activity can come up anytime in the future and can even affect one's prospects when it is time to interview for jobs or start a career.

You also want to think about the future. Many things people post online never really go away. This is true even if they are posted on sites or apps that promise that the content will eventually be deleted. In many cases, there is still an electronic footprint of that post somewhere out there that someone could eventually come across. Such posts have a tendency to coming back to haunt internet users later on in life, even years later. Something shared today could come back two or twenty years later to make one's life miserable or derail one's dreams. Inappropri-

YOU'RE ACCEPTED! ... OR NOT?

Imagine what it would be like to get accepted to an Ivy League school for college, only to have that acceptance rescinded a short time later. In 2017, that's exactly what happened to ten incoming Harvard University freshmen. Students communicating on a Facebook group posted inappropriate, offensive, and obscene memes on the group wall and within group chats.

These memes targeted racial groups, made jokes about the Holocaust, and mocked issues like sexual

A student strolls the Harvard University campus. Harvard is one of many schools that look into students' social media usage when considering candidates for acceptance.

assault, according to an article by Laura Krantz for the *Boston Globe.* Some may have done so because they truly thought it was funny to do so or simply to fit in and go with the flow.

Harvard's policy is that admission can be revoked for a number of reasons, including behavior "that brings into question their honesty, maturity, or moral character." The students at Harvard agree to abide by an honor code that requires them to have good and virtuous behavior. Ultimately, armed with screenshots and other records, Harvard officials told ten of the students that they were no longer welcome to attend the university.

Some people felt Harvard's action was an attack on freedom of speech. On the other hand, people also felt that the university had made the correct decision. One student interviewed by the *Boston Globe* explained that while he was surprised that the students would do this, he really wasn't that much surprised. He had personally witnessed an increase in hate speech among high school students during his time in school. As a result, he felt many of his fellow students had become desensitized. "I am glad, though, that they did take some sort of strict action on it," he said, referring to Harvard administrators.

ate posts can resurface and prevent admission to college, negatively affect or ruin a career, or cause breakups in relationships—even marriages.

Universities and places of employment frequently search out candidates online to find out if what is reported on an application really matches who the person is behind the scenes. The president of the National

Even if you are hired, old internet posts, comments, or other activity can surface at any time and cost you your job or student status if they are controversial enough.

Association for College Admissions, Nancy Beane, explained in an article on National Public Radio (NPR) in 2017 that students need to be careful about what they say and do online and if they make mistakes (which we all can do), they need to own up to them.

TOO MUCH INFO

Another reason to think before you post is to protect your real identity. Some of the most basic rules include never posting your home address, don't tell the name of your school or the sports team you play on, don't list the name of your city, and don't give out your phone number or private email address. You should also avoid giving too many details about your likes and interests, the route you take home from school, and so forth. Even seemingly innocent comments can provide unsavory individuals with enough information to narrow down your location and possibly your identity.

You can't avoid the internet altogether, since that isn't practical in today's modern world. Almost everyone needs it for school and work, and it is a great tool to make connections with others others. Nowadays, deciding to log off forever is like saying, "No thank you. I'd rather not have running water or electricity." The internet is so ingrained in all of our lives, that it's very near impossible to live a modern life without it. However, think before you post and take necessary precautions to protect yourself and your identity in the online world.

You can help others do better and be safer in their online interactions, too. If your friend makes a mistake and posts information or photos that are too personal, alert your friend immediately of the dangers of such behavior. She or he may not have even thought too deeply about how posts could come back to haunt her or him. Most people don't want to purposely put themselves at risk. They do so usually because they are not aware of the risks of certain behavior. Being aware, alert, and up-to-date on potential internet risks will keep you, your family, and your friends safe online.

SOME POINTERS FOR ONLINE SAFETY

There are many things you can do online to keep your-self safe. Here are some of them:

1. **Adjust Your Privacy Settings**. Make sure your privacy settings on all of your devices and apps are at their highest level possible.
2. **Protect Your Passwords**. Never give out your password to anyone. Also, make sure you change your passwords often. Don't use your address, phone number, name or nickname, or other easily searched for information in it. Choosing a password that has a combination letters, numbers, and symbols helps prevent your password from getting hacked. Some websites even require them, and judge your password creation attempts on a scale—for example, from weak to strong.
3. **Only Friend Friends**. Do not accept friend requests on social media from people you don't know. Also, keep your social media posts private so that only your friends and family can see what you post.
4. **No Real Life Meet-Ups**. Unless you are positively sure of someone's identity and their intentions, you should not meet people you encounter online, especially alone. Remember that someone can pretend to be pretty much anyone. A sixteen-year-old might seem like the most easygoing, friendly person you ever met. Just keep in mind, however, that that new friend might not be a teenager at all.

Rigorous password security is necessary for anyone who wants to live, thrive, and survive online. Avoid amateur errors, like using your email address or first or last name.

Meeting an online stranger could put you at risk of being assaulted, or worse. Before even thinking about agreeing to such a meet-up, ask a trusted adult, including a parent, grandparent, teacher, or anyone with your best interests in mind, about the situation.

5. **Use a Virus Checker**. Make sure your computer or other electronic device is equipped with the most up-to-date virus checking software.

6. **Avoid Public Wi-Fi**. Be wary of using public Wi-Fi, especially if it doesn't require a password to log on. Any information sent via public Wi-Fi can potentially be scooped up by others monitoring or hacking these networks.

7. **Make Yourself as Stalker Proof as Possible**. Avoid publicly listing a phone number, address, or primary email address online, including on social media profiles. If necessary, create a separate email address for such purposes. If you live in a small town, you may also want to put down a near-by city as your location instead. It's much more difficult to find an individual in a city of millions than it is in a small town of one thousand people.

8. **Just Click Off**. If you happen to go on a site that is suspicious or inappropriate, click out immediately. Encourage your friends to do the same.

9. **Don't Become Desensitized**. The moment we no longer feel bad about seeing or doing something inappropriate online, we need to immediately evaluate our actions in accordance with our own ethics. This constant and consistent set of checks and balances will allow our real-life ethics to de-termine our behavior—which will ultimately keep us safe and smart online.

Criminals, including burglars and even sexual predators, have been known to stalk their victims via social media posts—for example, ones declaring plans to be on vacation or alone at home.

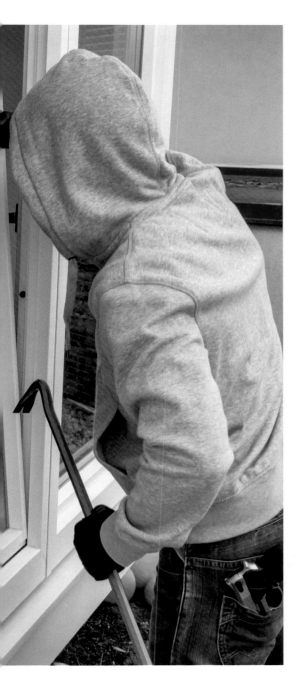

10. **Don't Reveal Travel Plans**. Some people like to share travel photos when they are on vacation. By doing so, people put themselves at risk. One risk is burglary and theft. For example, if an unscrupulous person online figures out that a family is out of town and already knows where that family lives, this person can break into the house while the family is gone. Instead, wait until you're home to post vacation photos and avoid "checking in" at locations since this also alerts crafty individuals to when you're not at home.

CHAPTER FOUR

DIGITAL ETHICS AND THE LAW

T he branch of the legal system that deals specifically with online activities and behavior is called internet law. There are still many debates about the effectiveness of internet laws. On one hand, some argue that it's impossible to truly regulate the internet. The vast realms of cyberspace have few enforceable physical, political, or geographic boundaries. Some nations have laws that prohibit certain activities while others do not. Cybercriminals, trolls, and hackers will often manipulate loopholes and varying standards, set up offshore accounts, host on foreign servers, and make other efforts to circumvent the rules.

On the other hand, some insist that the internet most certainly can be regulated, and many regulatory parameters having already been set. While it's true that some laws do exist to govern online behavior, these laws frequently lag behind the swift advances of technology. Internet laws have difficulty keeping up with the ever-changing world of the internet. When new technology, apps, or platforms are created, they present new

Many disagreements on what constitutes harassment, abuse, or simply unethical behavior online are settled in the courts, both civil and criminal.

problems that have to be considered on both ethical and legal bases. While it is challenging to enforce online standards and laws, it is certainly not impossible.

PROHIBITING ONLINE ABUSES

Many states have laws that protect people from online abuse, including harassment, cyberstalking, and cyber-bullying. Some of these are additions to the harassment, stalking, and bullying statutes that are already on the books. Consequences for breaking these laws vary by state and by the seriousness of the offense. In serious situations, perpetrators can face jail time, fines, and restriction of their internet access and usage.

The prevalence of online bullying has inspired students and adults to raise awareness and take action, like these students in 2013 at Katherine Edwards Middle School in Whittier, California.

The Cyberbullying Research Center website has a detailed chart on its "Bullying Laws Across America" page. This chart briefly explains the types of laws that each state has and includes links to the actual statutes. WHOA (Working to Halt Online Abuse) is another website that provides links to laws prohibiting such abuses, both in the United States and internationally. Those who believe their own state does not have adequate protections against cyber abuse can contact their state lawmakers. They can write letters and emails, make phone calls, or visit the relevant offices in person to engage their legislators and other officials. Keeping such legislation current is an important way of combating bullying and other forms of harassment.

Some of the earlier laws prohibiting cyber abuses protected only minors—individuals under the age of eighteen. Fortunately, lawmakers have reconsidered this restriction and have opened up the laws in most states to protect people of all ages. Cyberstalking, cyber harassing,

Acting silly or crazy for selfies is all in good fun. Make sure, however, that you don't get carried away and end up taking a picture that you cannot explain away later.

and cyberbullying do not have age restrictions. Everyone can be affected by such behavior. Many adults become victims of this type of treatment and also need to be protected by the law.

SCHOOLS GET INVOLVED

Many states require schools and school districts to establish rules that prohibit bullying and cyberbullying behavior. One of the primary duties of educators is keeping students safe. As a result, some schools have strict zero-tolerance policies. That means that if there is evidence of one student bullying others (either in person or online), that student could be suspended or expelled. In serious situations, the school may not have any recourse but to turn the case over to law enforcement.

It's important to note that bullying need not be between students. A student who makes inappropriate or offensive comments or threats online directed towards teachers, coaches, or school administration can also be disciplined for cyberbullying behavior. Firm punishment might not merely apply to things that happen only on school grounds. According to the Cyberbullying Research Center, "federal case law allows schools to discipline students for off-campus behavior that results in a substantial disruption of the learning environment at school."

REACHING OUT TO GET HELP

If a person feels that he or she is being threatened or abused online, his or her first step should be to confide in someone about it. While talking to a friend one's age is a good start, a trusted adult might be a better bet. Online communities and telephone hotlines can be great resources if a person feels that he or she wants to talk to someone off the record about the situation, especially anonymously.

For instance, Teen Line is an organization that provides teenagers with a chance to talk to other teens about situations they may be facing. The volunteers have been trained to help callers in all kinds of situations, including online mistreatment. Teens can text, call, or email to talk to a volunteer in real time. All conversations are kept anonymous.

There are also apps that provide help for teens who need to report incidences of cyberbullying, harassment, or even threats to individuals or the school in general. The state of Utah has an app called SafeUtah App. This app allows students and adults to report such issues anonymously. The app also provides a way for teens to talk to a real person about online or real-life issues that they might be facing twenty-four hours a day, seven days a week. The professionals on the other end of the call or text are trained in crisis management, suicide prevention, and dealing with bullying, threats, or violence. Other states, schools, and organizations likely have similar apps, too. Search online or in the app store to find ones with good ratings that you can utilize when needed.

It's important for the person being bullied to remember that it is not his or her fault. He or she does not deserve this type of treatment. It is the bully who is in the wrong. On the Pacer Center's Teens Against Bullying website, teens provide advice and words of encouragement to victims of bullying. Jessica, a seventeen-year-old from Michigan, stated:

> "No one in this world ever deserves to be bullied and brought down by people. And no one deserves to hold in all those situations that have happened to them. If you are being bullied open up and talk about it. I know it is hard to do but you are not alone. Others get bullied and know how you feel. People love you and will listen to you and be there for you. Stand up against bullying today."

INAPPROPRIATE PHOTOS

Many states have laws that prohibit minors from sending inappropriate, intimate photos of themselves or others in any electronic format. Most commonly known as sexting, the punishment for this type of activity varies by state. In some states, the first offense is a misdemeanor while subsequent offenses are felonies. Felonies are serious offenses and can lead to jail time.

Some teens think that sending these types of photos are fashionable, funny, or "just what people do." But the consequences in engaging in this type of behavior are severe and can land a person in a lot more trouble than they ever imagined. It can be terribly embarrassing, spark possible harassment from peers, and also get the sender (and even the receiver) in serious trouble with the law. While many advocates have started to push back on some of these harsh laws—especially extremely punitive ones that land more or less harmless teens on sexual offender registries, or in prison—teens should be aware of what they could be getting into by sexting.

LET'S BE HONEST

Ethical behavior on the internet also includes being honest and truthful in all of your activities, including the ways you use the materials you find online. Most people understand that walking into a store and taking whatever they want is not only illegal, but also unethical. A similar number of people also realize that taking someone else's term paper and printing it with their own name at the top is plagiarism, and therefore an ethical breach.

However, sometimes it's difficult to see online activities in the same way. If a friend posts a media file online, is it okay to download it? Is that taking something that doesn't belong to you, that you haven't paid for? Technically the song doesn't belong to your friend, but rather it belongs to the band that created it, or the record company or streaming service that distributes it. The same rules apply to videos, artwork, and photos. It also applies to copying and pasting information you find online into the paper you're writing for school and pretending those words are your own.

While illegal downloads of creative content, like one's favorite music, are on a sharp decline, be mindful that you consume media responsibly and honestly.

Many people who commit ethical breaches legitimately don't realize that their actions might be considered wrong. However, ethical standards and actual laws say otherwise. Videos, music, text, photos, artwork, and so forth can all fall under the category of intellectual property. Copyrighted materials belong to others and are protected by law.

Of course, this doesn't mean that you can't use any materials online since they belong to someone else. You just need to do so in an ethical way. This will not only help develop your character as an honest person, but it will also help prevent you from getting in trouble with the law.

Research carefully what content you can or cannot use in different contexts, whether it is for a presentation, a video project uploaded to YouTube, or something you intend to profit from.

KNOW THE RULES

Laws are updated all the time and can sometimes vary by where you live. Therefore, it's important that you stay up-to-date on what is legally allowed with intellectual property found online.

FILE DOWNLOADING AND FILE SHARING

According to current US federal laws, it is illegal to download software, movies, and music without paying for them. The consequences can be stiff: jail time and up to $150,000 per file according to the Digital Millennium Copyright Act. The best way to avoid this is to use only material that you have paid for. Or sign up for a music sharing or video sharing service that allows you to access the media in a legal fashion. With these streaming apps (Spotify, Hulu, Amazon Prime, and Netflix are examples), you can listen to music and watch television or movies either for free or for a small monthly fee. You can also rent movies from many of these streaming services. Since you're not downloading and "owning" any of these movies, you are allowed to watch them just as if you were viewing them on the television. It's the downloading and distributing of the material without paying for it that can land you in trouble.

AVOIDING PLAGIARISM

It's always best to use one's own words instead of someone else's when you write. Just think of how you would feel if you came up with an original story and someone else put his or her name on it and pretended it was his or hers. It would be upsetting, wouldn't it? When quoting information in research papers, always make sure you place quotation marks around the parts that another person said. And give the person who said it the proper credit. For more information on how to avoid plagiarism when writing, conduct an online search ("how to avoid plagiarism" is one phrase to use) to get the latest tips from experts.

USING IMAGES AND ART

Images, photographs, and other art forms are also protected under copyright law. You must have permission to use such materials. You can't put them on your own website, blog, promotional materials, or videos without permission from the creator. There are places where you can find free art that is in the public domain. Or you can purchase art for limited use from stock illustration, art, and photo websites. Conduct an online search to find some of the best current options.

CHAPTER FIVE

DIGITAL ETHICS AND YOU

Online activities can present challenges for many internet users as they figure out how to be good digital citizens. Every day that one goes online, there are opportunities to either contribute to hate and negativity or become a vehicle for positivity and enlightenment. We also have a choice about how we exhibit our *real* character online. How we show our integrity, our moral compass, our ethics—it's all up to us.

MAKING THE DECISION AHEAD OF TIME

By establishing a strong ethical foundation in our real life, we can easily make correct decisions online. If we make the decision ahead of time that we'll only behave in a certain way (no matter what situation we find ourselves in), then the in-the-moment decisions will be much easier because they'll have already been made in advance.

When a good digital citizen sees that a person is being cyberbullied, he or she will not join in. He or she

Teens need not make hard or confusing ethical choices about online actions in a vacuum. Parents and other trusted aduts are there to help.

also won't sit around and watch it happen. Instead, the good digital citizen will hopefully stand up and speak out in defense of that person or at least try to ease the situation. If he or she knows the person in real life, whether a good friend or even an acquaintance, he or she can befriend the cyberbullied person, leave nice notes for him or her in his or her locker, make sure he or she has someone to sit by at lunch, and ensure that

that person knows he or she has someone to rely on. We can be that person for someone else. We can make a difference.

A strong ethical foundation can guide teens in their online activity. For example, when someone asks us to send him or her an inappropriate photo of ourselves, we can politely let that person know that we don't do those kinds of things. When someone sends a mean or inappropriate photo of a classmate, the ethical teen can refrain from sharing it. If he or she is feeling bold, the ethical teen might even directly message the sender to reprimand him or her. When he or she finds information online to use for a school paper, he or she can make sure not to use any online sources without giving proper credit to the authors.

In another vein, when parents set rules for online behavior, a teen needs to rely on his or her judgment to try to adhere to those rules. For example, parents might not be happy with the types of conversations their child is having online or the types of photos he or she is circulating, if they were aware of them. Imagine that, instead of being sincere and owning up to questionable behavior, a teen instead hunts down an app or software that hides certain types of online activity. Concealing one's behavior should certainly tug at one's conscience. Instead, he or she should make the commitment ahead of ahead of time to act appropriately online because it's the right thing to do. A teen making that commitment can be proud of going the extra mile and building the character that will help them negotiate the online world.

TECHNOLOGY CONSUMPTION

Another aspect of modern digital life that worries some people is how hyperconnected many people are, including teenagers. Many digital natives (those who have never known a world without the internet) today spend much of their day fixated on screens or electronic devices of one kind or another. They spend many of their waking hours online: playing games, scrolling through social media, listening to music, watching videos, or texting with friends. Some of those activities even eke over into the middle of the night when the person should be sleeping.

While all of those activities can be fine in small doses, they are hardly a healthy way for people to spend all of their time. Often, the more time people spend online, the less connected they feel with the real world and the people in it. When going online is dominated by engaging on social media, for example, many people may feel more alienated and alone than when they log off for a time. Spending time offline and making connections with real people is crucial for anyone's overall well-being.

LISTEN TO THE EXPERTS

Did you know that Steve Jobs, the founder of Apple, had strict rules with his kids regarding their use of technology and the internet? The same goes for other technology entrepreneurs and executives. These people

Spending a healthy amount of time offline is a good way to maintain perspective, connect with others outside of social media, have fun, and preserve one's empathy for others.

often limit the amount of time that their children and teens can spend on their devices. They also limit or bar internet-connected screens (phones, computers, tablets, and so forth) in bedrooms and other places where they can be used in isolation, without supervision.

It is unsurprising that the people who created the devices and platforms we all use nowadays would be worried about their own children abusing them. After all, they know the pros and cons of these technologies better than almost anyone, including the perils of becoming addicted to being perpetually online. For instance, Sean Parker, a founding president of Facebook and a coinventor of the first widespread file-sharing platform, Napster, admitted in a video interview on the

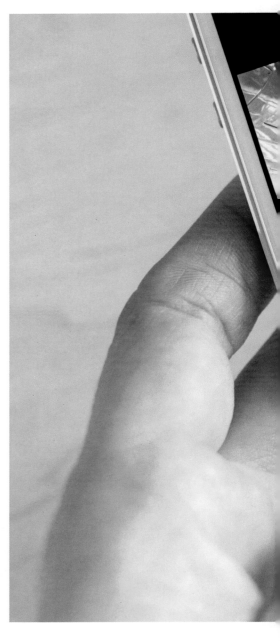

Technology companies like Facebook have spent millions—even billions—of dollars trying to figure how to make their platforms easy to use and addictive.

news network Axios that social media platforms are actually designed to become addictive. The developers consider this fundamental question when designing the platforms: How do we consume as much of your time and conscious attention as possible? They do this by exploiting a key element of human psychology: the need for validation.

By including the Like button or the comment feature, they actually give the human brain a little "hit of dopamine" every time the user sees that someone has liked or commented on his or her post. This natural "high" that the user experiences encourages him or her to get on again and again to check out how many more people have liked or commented on the post. It also encourages users to post more often so they can get additional validation. We all want to be liked and accepted by others. The developers of social media use this knowledge of human nature to make their platforms something people couldn't live without.

UNPLUGGING ON OCCASION

Knowing that people can become addicted to technology and the internet and abuse their status as digital citizens, how can we personally resolve their usage in our own lives? After all, we don't want to allow a device or platform to end up controlling our lives to the point that we end up like mindless zombies mesmerized by a glowing screen akin to something from a science fiction novel. Instead, we want

THE NEED FOR CHIEF ETHICISTS

Many experts believe that digital and tech companies need to hire chief ethicists to guide the company's decision making process. Among internet companies, in particular, the attitude can sometimes be that they'll develop the new platform, release it, and fix any problems that arise afterwards. But this method doesn't always work well from a moral standpoint. What happens when the platform is used for nefarious or criminal activity? It's too late to "fix" the platform when people have already been harmed by it.

Don Heider is the Founder of the Center for Digital Ethics & Policy at Loyola University. In an article he wrote for *USA Today* in January 2017, he argues that internet and social media companies need to hire chief ethicists to help them determine the moral ramifications of their ideas before they are released to the public. He explained, "Chief ethicists could help executives think through difficult, critical decisions. They could help develop ethical guidelines for companies, even a code of ethics. And they could provide company-wide training on ethical decision-making."

Instead of hiring people, though, sometimes these companies choose to allow computer algorithms to determine the company's course of action. But many would argue that while computers can be used to determine if something can be done, they certainly cannot be used to determine if something should be done. The moral compass and ethics needed to make such determinations are only found within the minds and hearts of humans.

to use them for good purposes where they benefit our real lives, not take over our real lives.

Take the time to consider your own personal ethics in regards to how much time you should be spending on your devices and what you could choose to do instead. Do you want to be so focused on an electronic screen that you miss out on everything physically around you in the real world? A recommendation: take time to get outside and enjoy the beauty of nature, listen to people when they talk, explore other interests, try out some new hobbies that don't involve technology, just simply look at the real world around you and see

Being good digital citizens by acting ethically online will make things better for everyone and create a community that most people can feel safe in and engaged with.

how different you will start to feel. This recommendation is meant for everyone, not just kids and teens, since the addictive nature of technology and online platforms can affect all ages.

Just remember that ethics has to do with "should" versus "can." Just because you can spend every second of your day online, doesn't mean that you should. Unplugging on occasion is actually a really good thing. It will give you time to figure out who you are and the person you want to become. That knowledge will further serve you in your real-world and online-world experiences.

Everyone has the opportunity in their daily usage of the internet to make an impact on digital ethics. The choices that each individual makes are like strokes of paint on a grand masterpiece. Each stroke, each choice, helps determine whether or not the finished painting is something beautiful and pleasing to the eye. By developing our real-life ethics and then applying those principles to our online activities, we can make sure that our contributions help the internet be a positive and impactful place for everyone who uses it, including ourselves.

ACTIVITIES

Activity 1
Ethics Survey
Individuals or teams are assigned to do an informal and anonymous internet survey, using contacts from their email lists, or social media, and a free survey site like Surveymonkey.com.
- Recipients of the survey are asked whether they have ever done anything questionable online that fits any of the many categories of ethical breaches listed in this work.
- Survey respondents are asked to classify these according to type.
- Respondents also are questioned on whether they have ever had an ethical breach online affect them negatively. How so?
- Those conducting the survey gather the responses, classify them, and tabulate them.
- Those participating in this activity then combine their efforts and issue a report and presentation on digital ethics, revealing their complete findings.
- They discuss these findings in a group and determine how to use the various safeguards within this work to prevent future breaches.

Activity 2
Ethics: Going Global
Members of the classroom are divided up into groups and are assigned different nations at random from around the world in order to explore any global differences when it comes to digital ethics. They can explore how different people worldwide deal with:

- Securing their financial and personal information.
- Their approaches to what they share and how these might differ among cultures, even among different cultures living in the same nation.

Sources can include articles online, digital ethics organizations who have researched such matters, personal anecdotes from friends or relatives living overseas, or even digital pen pals who are engaged respectfully via social media, comment boards, or other online spaces

Students regroup after their research and formulate a system of scoring nations, continents, regions, cultures, etc., on how strictly or seriously they consider digital ethics and safety in their day-to-day interactions. This gives students a taste of how digital citizenship plays out among members of their age cohort all around the world.

Activity 3
Brainstorming Ethics

Students brainstorm incidents in their experience and recent histories when they were presented with dilemmas or questions about how to live their online lives ethically and safely. These may include:

- Choosing to engage in—or disengage from—bullying, trolling, harassing, or internet pile-ons
- Whether to post a picture or not, if it revealed too much about oneself, or put others at risk of harassment, doxxing, or other negative feedback
- Balancing sharing fun stories, pictures, and experiences, versus putting too much out there that would give potential predators too much information
- Befriending strangers online, and deciding whether to deepen such relationships by revealing personal info, or even meeting up in person

GLOSSARY

anonymously Doing something without revealing one's own real identity.

cyberbullying The repeated hurting, threatening, or intimidating of another person by an individual or group of people in an online environment.

desensitized Becoming unfeeling to something or unaffected by something that should normally make one feel certain emotions.

doxxing The malicious intent of searching out the private information of someone and then publishing that information online.

ethos A Greek term that refers to a custom, habit, character, or disposition. It is the basis of the word "ethics."

ethics A word that stems from the Greek word *ethos.* This term refers to a person's moral, internal principles that govern their behavior.

expelled When someone is kicked out of school.

golden rule The principle that one should do unto others as they would want others to do unto them.

identity theft When someone gets his or her personal identity stolen, such as his or her name, social security number, credit card numbers, and so forth. With this information, someone can open up accounts in that person's name.

intellectual property A work that is made using some form of creativity. Inventions, writing, music, art, photographs, and so forth fall under the umbrella of intellectual property.

moral compass An inner guide that helps a person determine right from wrong.

navigate To make one's way through something, as a sailor finds his or her way across the sea by using special tools and astronomical methods.

netizens People who participate in any way on the internet.

philosophy A branch of study that deals with the fundamental nature of knowledge.

protagonists The main character in a book, movie, story, who is generally the "good guy" in contrast to the "bad guy," villain, or antagonist.

screenshots A photograph taken of information on a person's screen that is taken by the device that contains the screen.

sexting The sending of intimate photos of oneself or others in any electronic format.

streaming A way to transmit or receive video or audio files as a steady, continuous flow.

trolling A behavior that includes leaving antagonistic or offensive comments on posts in order to cause contention amongst users in a community.

unscrupulous Dishonest, unethical, or immoral.

FOR MORE INFORMATION

Center for Digital Ethics & Policy
Loyola University
1032 West Sheridan Road
Chicago, IL 60660
Website: http://www.digitalethics.org
Twitter: @digethics
This center is part of the School of Communication at
Loyola University. The purpose of the center is to pro-
vide a way for people to discuss issues of digital ethics
and conduct related research. The center provides a
course and certification program in digital ethics.

Pacer's National Bullying Prevention Center
80 East Hillcrest Drive, #203
Thousand Oaks, CA 91360
Website: http://www.pacer.org/bullying
Facebook and Twitter: @Pacercenter
The mission of the Pacer Center, founded in 2006, is
to encourage changes in society so "bullying is no
longer considered an accepted childhood rite of
passage." Pacer Center provides resources for students, teachers, and schools.

PrevNet, Canada
c/o PREVNet Administrative Centre
Queen's University
98 Barrie Street
Kingston, ON

K7L 3N6
Canada
(613) 533-2632
Website: https://www.prevnet.ca
Facebook, Instagram, and Twitter: @prevnet
PrevNet is an acronym that stands for "Promoting Relationships and Eliminating Violence Network." This Canadian organization's main goal is to stop all bullying in Canada. They provide resources for parents, children, teachers, and media.

Project Zero: The Good Play Project
c/o Harvard Graduate School of Education
13 Appian Way
Cambridge, Massachusetts 02138
Website: http://www.pz.harvard.edu/projects/the-good
-play-project
Facebook and Twitter: @ProjectZeroHGSE
This organization focuses on the digital ethical education for youth and includes interviews with young people, parents, and teachers on such topics as freedom of speech, privacy, property, and identity in an online environment. It also includes a curriculum called Our Space which teachers can use in the classroom to teach important ethical topics.

StopBullying.gov
US Department of Health and Human Services
200 Independence Avenue SW
Washington, DC 20201
Website: https://www.stopbullying.gov

Facebook: @StopBullying.Gov

The Stop Bullying campaign aims to educate youth and adults about specific topics related to bullying. Its staff works with the US Department of Education to create policy, conduct research, and develop materials related to these topics.

Teen Line
Cedars-Sinai
PO Box 48750
Los Angeles, CA 90048-0750
Website: https://teenlineonline.org
Facebook and Twitter: @teenlineonline

Teen Line was founded in 1980. Its goal is to connect at-risk teens with trained teen volunteers.

FOR FURTHER READING

Baym, Nancy K. *Personal Connections in the Digital Age* (Digital Media and Society). Cambridge, UK: Polity Press, 2015.

Cover, Rob. *Digital Identities: Creating and Communicating the Online Self.* Waltham, MA: Academic Press, 2016.

Davisson, Amber, and Paul Booth. *Controversies in Digital Ethics.* New York, NY: Bloomsbury Academic, 2016.

Kamberg, Mary-Lane. *Cybersecurity: Protecting Your Identity and Data.* New York, NY: Rosen Central, 2018.

Meeuwisse, Raef. *Cybersecurity for Beginners.* Canterbury, UK: Lulu Publishing, 2015.

Pojman, Louis P., and James Feiser. *Ethics: Discovering Right and Wrong.* Boston, MA: Wadsworth Publishing, 2016.

Price, Catherine. *How to Break Up with Your Phone: The 30-Day Plan to Take Back Your Life.* New York, NY: Random House, 2018.

Quinn, Michael J. *Ethics for the Information Age.* New York, NY: Pearson, 2016.

Shafer-Landau, Russ. *The Ethical Life: Fundamental Readings in Ethics and Contemporary Moral Problems.* Oxford, England: Oxford University Press, 2017.

Vanacker, Bastiaan, and Don Heider. *Ethics for a Digital Age.* New York, NY: Peter Lang Publishing, 2015.

BIBLIOGRAPHY

Academic Earth. "The Psychology of the Internet Troll."
     Retrieved March 11, 2018. http://academicearth.org
     /electives/psychology-internet-troll.
Allen, Mike. "Sean Parker Unloads on Facebook:
     'God Only Knows What it's Doing to Our Children's
     Brains'." Axios, November 9, 2017. https://www
     .axios.com/sean-parker-unloads-on-facebook
     -god-only-knows-what-its-doing-to-our-childrens
     -brains-1513306792-f855e7b4-4e99-4d60-8d51
     -2775559c2671.html.
Barrett, Natasha. "Mystery Student Using Social Media
     for Good Reveals Herself." ABC 13, September 29,
     2014. http://abc13.com/technology/mystery-student
     -using-social-media-for-good-reveals-her
     -self/329458.
Bilton, Nick. "Steve Jobs Was a Low-Tech Parent."
     New York Times, September 10, 2014. https://www
     .nytimes.com/2014/09/11/fashion/steve-jobs-apple
     -was-a-low-tech-parent.html.
Burroughs, Michael D. "The Significance of Ethics and
     Ethics Education in Daily Life." TedXTalks, April 4,
     2016. https://www.youtube.com/watch?v=_8juebyo
     _Z4.
Cyberbullying Research Center. "Bullying Across Ameri-
     ca." Retrieved March 12, 2018. https://cyberbullying.
     org/bullying-laws.
Cyberbullying Research Center. "State Cyberbullying
     Laws." Retrieved March 12, 2018. https://cyberbullying
     .org/Bullying-and-Cyberbullying-Laws.pdf.

Green, Lee. "Cyberbullying: Challenging Legal Issues for Schools." National Federation of State High School Associations, February 10, 2016. https://www.nfhs.org/articles/cyberbullying -challenging-legal-issues-for-schools.

Heider, Don. "Why Facebook Should Hire a Chief Ethicist." *USA Today,* January 8, 2017. https://www .usatoday.com/story/opinion/2017/01/08/facebook -ethics-fake-news-social-media-column/96212172.

Kamanetz, Anya. "Harvard Rescinds Admission of 10 Students Over Obscene Facebook Messages." NPR, June 6, 2017. https://www.npr.org/sections /ed/2017/06/06/531591202/harvard-rescinds -admission-of-10-students-over-obscene -facebook-messages.

Krantz, Laura. "Harvard Revokes Admission to at Least 10 Students for Offensive Facebook Posts." *Boston Globe,* June 5, 2017. https://www.bostonglobe .com/lifestyle/2017/06/05/harvard-revokes -admission-least-students-for-offensive-facebook -posts/kl0icc1doFDmWlg3T6dKCJ/story.html.

Pacer Center Teen's Against Bullying. "Cyberbullying." Retrieved March 2, 2018. https://www.pacerteensagainstbullying.org /experiencing-bullying/cyber-bullying.

Retter, Emily. "Billionaire Tech Mogul Bill Gates Reveals He Banned his Children from Mobile Phones Until They Turned 14." *The Mirror*, April 21, 2017. https://www.mirror.co.uk/tech/billionaire-tech-mogul -bill-gates-10265298.

Webster University. "Illegal Downloading." Retrieved March 3, 2018. http://www.webster.edu/technology /service-desk/illegal-downloading.html.

Williams, Terri. "The Role of Social Media in Adolescent/Teen Depression and Anxiety." Center for Digital Ethics and Policy, April 3, 2018. http://www.digitalethics.org/essays /role-social-media-adolescentteen-depression -and-anxiety.

INDEX

A

Amazon Prime, 53
anonymity, pros and cons of, 26–27
art/images, using, 54
Axios, 62

B

Back to the Future, 19
Beane, Nancy, 35
Boston Globe, 33
bullying, 17–20
"Bullying Laws Across America," 45
business ethics, 9

C

catfishing, 20
Center for Digital Ethics & Policy, 63
chief ethicists, 63
copyright, 51, 53, 54
cyberbullying, 20–23
    combating, 22–23
    how to not do it, 29
    laws prohibiting, 43–47
    reading out for help to survive, 48–49
    school policies against, 47

Cyberbullying Research Center, 45, 47
cybercriminals, 42
cyber harassment, 5
    laws prohibiting, 43–47
cyberstalking, laws prohibiting, 43–47

D

digital community, 13–16
digital ethics
    and art/media consumption, 50–51, 53–54
    definition, 11
    keeping up with tech developments, 12–13
    questions related to, 11–12
    think before you post, 29, 30–35, 55–57
Digital Millennium Copyright Act, 53
digital natives, 6, 58
dopamine, 62
doxxing, 21
drones, ethical use of, 14

E

ethics
    in different fields, 9–11
    purpose of, 7–9
    word origin, 7

ABOUT THE AUTHOR

Amie Jane Leavitt graduated from Brigham Young University and is an accomplished author, researcher, and photographer. She has written multiple books for youth, contributed to online and print media, and worked as a consultant, writer, and editor for numerous educational publishing and assessment companies.

PHOTO CREDITS